MEMORIES
OF A CIVIL ENGINEER IN
THE
PACIFIC NORTHWEST

MEMORIES OF A CIVIL ENGINEER IN THE PACIFIC NORTHWEST

BY

MARVIN RUNYAN

www.bookstandpublishing.com

Published by
Bookstand Publishing
Morgan Hill, CA 95037
3776_6

Copyright © 2012 by Marvin Runyan
All rights reserved. No part of this publication may be reproduced or transmitted in any form or by any means, electronic or mechanical, including photocopy, recording, or any information storage and retrieval system, without permission in writing from the copyright owner.

ISBN 978-1-61863-399-6

Printed in the United States of America

ACKNOWLEDGEMENTS

To my wife Julia who gave me her unqualified support during 58 years of happy marriage.

INTRODUCTION

I retired as President and CEO of STRAAM in Portland, Oregon on July 1, 1979. STRAAM was the successor of a merger with Stevens, Thompson & Runyan, Inc. of which I was President and CEO. I started with the company in 1940 when it was Stevens & Koon. Upon my retirement Jim Jordan of the Daily Journal of Commerce wrote an article about my career accomplishments in his column "Bulldozing".

Thirty two years later I was contacted by Bennett Johnson from the Portland Downtown Rotary Club requesting information about my career as a Civil Engineer. She had been writing about Rotarians who have been in the club for more than 30 years. I have been an active member for over 40 years. I put together extensive background information for her and was honored by her presentation to the club in November, 2011. Afterwards I met and shook hands with several young engineers who thanked me for my part in engineering the infrastructure of the Pacific Northwest. Although I have said many times that I would never write a book, the seed was planted.

Having been blessed with good health for 94 years, it was quite a setback when I was diagnosed, early in 2012, with a bacterial blood infection which kept me in the hospital and the Willamette View Health Center for considerable time. As my recovery progressed so did my boredom. I began making notes about milestones in my career and thinking back to my early years and experiences as a Civil

Engineer. It occurred to me that telling my life story in my own words would be a legacy that my family would someday appreciate. Throughout my career I had written countless reports which generally outlined technical answers to engineering problems. I realized that my life indeed had something in common with these reports - finding solutions to problems - and so I began writing this book. I don't know if bringing back old memories helped but I have since recovered and continue to enjoy life.

TABLE OF CONTENTS

Acknowledgements		v
Introduction		vii
Chapter 1	Willamette, Oregon	1
Chapter 2	El Cerrito, California	7
Chapter 3	Mulino, Oregon	11
Chapter 4	My College Years	19
Chapter 5	Reflections on My Early Years	25
Chapter 6	Stevens & Koon	27
Chapter 7	Fort Leonard Wood & Southern California	35
Chapter 8	Kiska	39
Chapter 9	Oahu	43
Chapter 10	Leyte	47
Chapter 11	Okinawa	51
Chapter 12	Reflections on the War Years	57
Chapter 13	Back to Work	61
Chapter 14	Stevens, Thompson, & Runyan	65
Chapter 15	Reflections on My Career	79
Chapter 16	Retirement	83
Chapter 17	Travel	87
Chapter 18	Reflections on My Retirement	91

Chapter 1

Willamette, Oregon

I know little about the very early years of the Runyan family except a few things that I have read and heard from others. It is my understanding that Vincent Rongnion of Poitiers, France was a French Huguenot who was fleeing religious persecution and escaped to the Isle of Jersey off the coast of France. From there he crossed the waters and in 1665 settled in what is now Elizabeth, New Jersey. Subsequently the name was spelled Runion and also Runnion and has been spelled Runyon and Runyan for nearly two centuries. Damon Runyon, whose stories were the basis for the musical "Guys and Dolls", was born Alfred Damon Runyan in Manhattan, Kansas in 1880. There is a story that when he was a young reporter a proofreader incorrectly edited the spelling of his name so Runyan became Runyon, a change he let stand. He dropped his first name when an editor told him "Damon Runyon" was a good-looking byline.

My father Albert Augustus Runyan was born in Thayer, Kansas on April 23, 1883. He was the eldest of two sons and one daughter born to Cyrus and Ella Runyan. His father was a blacksmith and part time preacher and his mother was a housewife.

Anna Elisabeth Larson, my mother, was born in Chicago, Illinois on October 13, 1891. She was the eldest of three daughters and a son born to Olof Larson and Bertha Person. Olof and Bertha emigrated from Sweden shortly after they were married. While first in Chicago Olof did odd jobs and Bertha did housework to make a living. They soon moved to a farm in Clintonville, Wisconsin and later to Princeton, Minnesota. In 1908 the family moved to Willamette, Oregon, a small community near Oregon City. Olof found work at the paper mill in nearby West Linn and was employed there until he retired.

My father started working at the paper mill at a young age after grade school. He and my mother were married on June 18, 1916. By the time I was born, February 17, 1918, my father had a good job as a machinist and millwright. We lived in a nice neighborhood in a comfortable house which had a yard with large fir trees. These trees dropped lots of fir needles and one of my first memories is filling my coverall pockets with as many fir needles as possible and seeing how far I could throw them up in the air.

Willamette was a close-knit community and to a large degree it was a mill town. The Willamette Pulp & Paper Mill was built in 1889.

It merged with Crown Columbia in 1914 to become the Crown-Willamette Paper Company and merged again in 1928 with Zellerbach Paper Company of San Francisco to become Crown-Zellerbach. Not only did my father work at the mill but my mother's father was a night watchman. My mother's two sisters and a brother lived in Willamette as well as my father's mother and her second husband. My sister Evelyn was born on December 10, 1919 and my brother Norman was born on May 16, 1927.

My mother was a very gentle woman and never was one to show anger or lose control. Her first concern was for her family and secondly for anyone who needed help. When I was quite young she developed a cough and a spot showed up on one of her lungs. There was concern it might turn into TB so special precautions had to be taken. Fortunately it never did.

My father was good about taking me to see interesting things. I remember going to the Portland harbor and seeing the Battleship Oregon which left a lasting memory. I also recall another time when we went to see what was then said to be the largest steam locomotive in the world. Another very favorite place was the zoo.

As a small boy I was of course interested in cowboys and Indians. I particularly liked western movies and my father occasionally took me to the Star Theater in Oregon City on Saturday afternoons. I well remember one such occasion when I became so enthralled with the action that I found myself standing up alone in the audience. This was the first time I felt real embarrassment.

A small friend and I used to play with a Colt 1851 Navy revolver that belonged to his grandfather who had been in the Civil War. One day we left it in the yard and it was stolen. I never forgot that gun.

I was very fond of pets. My first pet was a chipmunk and then one Easter I received a small rabbit. We had a lawn with lots of small white clover blossoms which the rabbit liked very much. My father made a moveable wire covered frame without a bottom so the rabbit could be in the cage and still eat the clover. This worked fine and all we had to do was move the frame after the rabbit ate the clover under it. Unfortunately, disaster occurred one night when a dog turned over the frame and killed my rabbit. I was very broken up about it and my parents bought me a banty hen and rooster to replace the rabbit. This worked fine for a time until they flew over the fence into the neighbor's garden and were quite unwelcome. My solution was to trade them to a friend for a pair of pigeons. These turned out to be homing pigeons which suddenly decided to go home. I learned something about trading early.

Leonard Runyan, my father's brother, owned Runyan's Jewelry Store in Vancouver, Washington. He, his wife and my five cousins lived on a small acreage near the city. He belonged to a riding club and kept several good horses to ride, one a beautiful Arabian. When we went to visit, it was always a thrill for me to ride Dusky, a large brown horse.

The riding club used English saddles but when I rode it was always with a cowboy saddle. One Sunday visit we arrived just as the club was disbanding from their Sunday ride and Dusky had on an English saddle. Not wanting to take the time to change saddles, my Uncle decided to leave it on Dusky and we took off on our ride. Everything went well with our ride until we reached the end. Dusky was more than ready to head for home and became almost impossible for me to control. I was all over the saddle and hanging on for dear life. We made it back, but that was the last time I ever used an English saddle.

My father's job as a millwright was quite important because it was necessary to keep all parts of the paper mill in operation. As I understand it, this required working directly in water quite a bit and was physically demanding. Over the years he had saved some money and was ready to make a change. Not long after I was born, he bought a piece of property in Willamette, built a nice store which included living quarters, and opened a grocery store. There was one other similar store in town.

This was before the large cash & carry supermarkets and before credit cards. Things went well for awhile. The Mill would pay the workers monthly and some would pay cash for groceries, while others might need credit during the month. No problem since they could pay up when they got their Mill check. However, the eventual arrival of the cash, low price stores like Piggly Wiggly began to hurt our business. When shoppers had cash they would go to those stores and when they needed credit, they would come to ours. As time went by, the competition became more and more difficult for small stores.

My father's sister Bertha and her husband, who was an artist and house painter, had an art store in Oakland California. She convinced my father things were better there and encouraged us to head south. At this time I was in the 4th grade just having finished the 3rd grade in my Aunt's classroom at Willamette Grade School. Up until then my life had been wonderful with lots of young friends plus grandparents, aunts, uncles and cousins always available on holidays. I hated to leave.

Chapter 2

El Cerrito, California

When we got to the San Francisco Bay area in 1928 it was quite a shock. It was totally different from what I had known in Willamette. My father found a vacant store for rent in El Cerrito not far from Oakland. He and my mother opened a variety store. It was located on a busy street with living quarters in the rear of the store. Commercial buildings surrounded the backyard which had a well and a tall windmill that furnished our water.

There were few children in the area that were the same age as Evelyn and I. However, my aunt, uncle and three cousins lived in Oakland which was not far away so we visited them often. My parents attended the Methodist Church in El Cerrito and my sister and I attended Sunday School.

We met many new people. I remember an old sailor who had been many places and would tell me about his adventures. To cap it off he gave me an old Colt Revolver that he had picked up. It had gone through the fire during the San Francisco Earthquake. It was ruined and rusty but still resembled what I had seen in the cowboy movies. This was my second experience with a Colt firearm and I kept it for quite awhile.

From an early age I liked to draw. The subjects usually included cowboys, Indians, sailboats, cars and cartoon figures which I drew on sheets of plain paper. (I don't know if this helped me when years later I had to draft my design plans).

I went to Harding Elementary School in El Cerrito. It was a ten block walk to school. There are two school experiences that I particularly remember. Not too long after starting school, the teacher selected about six of us to take a special exercise class to improve our posture. This embarrassed me to think I was such a slob. From then on every morning I would throw my shoulders back and breathe deeply as I walked the ten blocks to school. After several weeks when the class was over, I was awarded a small prize for having made the most improvement in my posture. (I don't know if it has lasted but in ROTC at one time I was appointed adjutant to take the first step in parades – I think because of posture). One other experience I clearly remember had to do with operating the traffic signal at the school during lunch and recess. I volunteered for this and ended up missing lots of recess play because of it. Even so, I liked my teachers and particularly my Principal. It was also the first time I remember girls being interested in me – especially one who used to try to catch me in the coat closet.

After finishing at Harding it was on to Longfellow Junior High School in Richmond where the best students went. This was some distance from El Cerrito and required a bus ride to and from. This meant there was little time for after school activities and I missed out on Junior High sports. Nevertheless, I liked my teachers and got good grades. I particularly liked my English teacher who read a poem in class which was the first time I heard it and it became my favorite.

On my birthday February 17, 1929, my young brother Norman died in the hospital from pneumonia. He was buried in a cemetery in Oakland. It was a very sad time and I doubt if my parents ever fully recovered. He was with us for such a short time that my memories are mostly from photo albums showing Norman with Evelyn and me.

The San Francisco Bay Area was a great place for a young boy. We did not have a car but bus and trolley lines provided good transportation. There were ferries to get across the Bay to see Golden Gate Park and other interesting sites in San Francisco and the surrounding area. I have pleasant memories of many things I experienced there during my childhood. Today many members of my family live in the Bay area.

Despite working very hard, things in the store were not going well and the Depression was approaching. My father's health was failing. He was not a large man but was stocky and had always been very active. He had been a good wrestler for his weight. However, he developed rheumatoid arthritis which caused swelling of his hands making it painful and difficult to work with them. Spending so many years at the paper mill as a millwright which required working in water on the machinery was suspected as a cause. There was no cure.

In 1932 it was decided to move back to Willamette. When we got there it was further decided that the best thing to do was to buy a small farm where we could raise food.

Chapter 3

Mulino, Oregon

It was now time for me to go to High School. I spent my first six months at West Linn High. Then my parents bought a seven acre farm at Mulino south of Oregon City. The property had a house, barn, some outbuildings and it was fenced. There were about two acres which had been used for pasture. It had not been cleared of brush and there were a few pine trees.

This was another completely new experience for me. I don't believe that my father found it very close to his machinist training either but he was very handy. He always insisted that everything had to be done with precision. Whenever I questioned him about jobs around the farm his response was, "If it's worth doing, it's worth doing right."

I started school at Molalla Union High School and found I was six months behind because they had started classes before West Linn. I had to work hard to catch up. Evelyn, my sister, went to grade school at Mulino. I went by bus to Molalla and she walked to school.

The house was well built and comfortable with two bedrooms, living room, kitchen, porches and attached storage room and outhouse. However, the rooms were quite small. There was a typical barn with a hay loft above the first floor and an open shed along one side. We did not have a car but there was a small grocery store nearby in Mulino.

Before long we had bought a cow, chickens, and a couple of pigs. When it came to farming we had to hire jobs such as plowing, planting, and wood cutting to be done by others who had the proper equipment. My father was limited to what he could do, but often did more than he should and my mother was a hard worker. We all pitched in. Evelyn helped my mother and I took the cow to the pasture, milked her, and fed her. I fed the chickens and pigs and did other chores. We also had a Manx cat.

We planted a garden with corn, potatoes and other things that we could grow on the size land we had. There was plenty to eat but nothing coming in. I became very discouraged. I was six months behind on schoolwork and I suggested that I quit school and get a job. Both of my parents flatly refused to listen to me. Neither of them had gone beyond grammar school. I then decided I would make the best of it and began to work hard catching up on my schoolwork. I found my teachers very helpful and before long I had caught up.

In the summer during harvest time there were opportunities for women and children to help make some money. There were strawberries, raspberries, hops, teasels, etc. to be picked. Men helped with hay bailing and threshing. My mother, sister, and I took advantage of this the first summer.

After my second year of high school, in the summer of 1934, a friend and I decided to get a job and earn some money. We heard that a farmer who raised teasels commercially was hiring men to hoe young teasel plants near Molalla about five miles from where we lived. At that time heads of teasel plants were harvested, dried, processed and then used to raise the nap on woolen material. It was said he was the only teasel grower west of the Mississippi.

My friend and I appeared on the front porch of a very large brick house early one morning and rang the bell. After a short time the door opened and a stern elderly Scotsman asked "what do you boys want?" We said we wanted a job hoeing teasels. He then said "I am hiring men not boys" and turned and went inside closing the door. Surprised, we didn't know what to do so we just stood there. After a few minutes the door opened a crack and he said "are you boys still here?" We said "yes and we want a job." After a little discussion he said he would send us out with his crew and if we could keep up he would give us a job and if not – no job, no pay.

We went out to a large field where about a dozen men were hoeing long rows of small plants led by the farmer's son. It was hot and he really set the pace to test us. We had to work hard to keep up but we did and at quitting time my friend and I raced out of the field to show off.

The job paid twenty cents per hour for ten hours a day working six days a week. After a week's work I earned twelve dollars. However, those were Depression times and some of the men on the crew were trying to support their entire family on this salary. During teasel harvest I got a job as basket carrier which paid thirty cents per hour. At harvest time the teasel plants after two years were five to six feet tall with multiple sticky heads. The pickers would cut the heads off with a palm knife and put them in a large basket. When the basket was full I would give them a ticket, put the basket on my shoulder and empty it in a wagon. It was like going through a field of large thistles to the wagon so heavy clothes were necessary even in the summer heat.

I learned a lot that first summer and each summer thereafter until I went to college I had a job in the teasel fields.

However, before my first season was finished in the teasel fields there was a problem. My friend left for another job and with him went his Model T Ford that we used for transportation. Our family had no car which was an ongoing problem. By this time I had earned some money so I decided to see if I could solve the problem. I went to Oregon City to Weiler Chevrolet one Saturday, told them my problem and asked if they could help. They showed me a 1927 blue Chevrolet touring car that was a basket case. Bad paint, broken running boards and dented body were topped by ragged side curtains and top. However, it ran and the price was $25.00 so I bought my first car. My Dad was very good at building and fixing things and he helped me with fixing it up. He replaced the running boards, we repainted it light blue and named it The Bluebird. He also made mechanical repairs as necessary. It kept my job and served us till we could get a better one later. I was always interested in mechanical things and my experiences with this old car resulted in my love for the automobile. When I was young and we were living in the grocery store, I could tell what car (Ford, Chevrolet, Dodge, etc.) was coming up the road by the sound of its engine

Since Molalla High School was about 5 miles from Mulino, a school bus had normally been used to transport the Mulino students to and from school. One year the school bus was cancelled and a transportation cost was paid to each student by the District. That year I transported a number of neighborhood kids in The Bluebird. I made $125 which was used for a new roof on our house.

In late 1935 I traded the 1927 Chevrolet (The Bluebird) for a 1928 Oakland Roadster. I found it in a used car lot in Portland. The list price was $85 but they allowed me $65 on the Chevrolet trade-in. The Roadster had a tan body with orange trim, dark brown fenders, and orange wire wheels with two spares in fender wells, tan soft top and a rumble seat. As the used car dealer said – a very "doggy"car.

This was an improvement over The Bluebird and it became the family car. I drove it to work in the summer, to school functions and had a lot of fun with it. However, in the Fall of 1936 when I was getting ready to go away to college, I realized that it would be cost prohibitive for me to keep it at school. Since I was the only driver in the family, I needed to sell it. Sadly, I peddled it to used car dealers and ended up getting less than I had paid for it.

I previously mentioned that my father's sister and her family lived in Oakland. Her husband was an artist and also a house painter. One summer he had some older houses to paint which needed considerable scraping for preparation. I took the train down and earned money scraping paint and had a good visit with my cousins.

Other summer family trips I remember fondly were to the Oregon coast at Pacific City. We would spend about a week and while there we hiked to Cape Kiwanda and fished for Sea Bass from the rocks. At that time there was no road on the beach to the cape from Pacific City so it was a long walk in the sand. We also did some clam digging and fishing along the Nestucca River.

Another summer my father worked for the owner of Wilhoit Springs and we camped there while he was working. There were several small trout streams where I could fish.

I also used to fish for Sun Fish on the Willamette River from openings in the log rafts. Other times a neighbor and I would row upriver to Rock Island and fish for Bass.

Milk Creek, a small stream, was not very far from the farm. Not long after we moved to Mulino an elderly bachelor built a small log cabin on the bank nearby. When he decided to move my father bought the property and the cabin. It was small and basic but well built and it was a nice place to have a summer picnic with family and friends. One winter there was enough ice on the creek for ice skating and I remember falling and bumping my eyebrow.

Further up the creek there was a good swimming hole. At that time there were no public pools anywhere close by or at the high school. In the summer I went to the swimming hole on Milk Creek and from my vantage point on the bank I watched the movements of the swimmers below. Then later I imitated them – dog paddle, side stroke, and butterfly. That is how I learned to swim.

Firearms always fascinated me. In High School I got a Winchester 22 rifle. In the area around the farm there were a number of squirrels and small animals. One sunny afternoon I went squirrel hunting. I saw a large squirrel and after taking careful aim, shot it. When it quit squirming I felt very sad. I never again shot an animal or a bird. This did not change my interest in firearms but only in hunting.

Chapter 4

My College Years

My sister Evelyn and I both did well in school. She was two years behind me. We lived about five miles from the high school and I had to take a bus which made it difficult to participate in after school activities. However, my biggest problem was that I wanted very much to play football and my father was adamantly against it. His position was that it was a dangerous sport and not worth the risk of a lifelong injury. I took an active part in other activities, got good grades and graduated in 1936 as Salutatorian of my class of 50 students. I also received a scholarship to Oregon State.

In those days going to college was rather rare in Molalla and only a few in my class planned to do so. It was a forestry and farming town and it was relatively easy to find work in one of these occupations. None of my older cousins from other areas had gone to college.

The prospect of living away from home was daunting and something I had never done. The scholarship covered college costs but how could I cover living costs and still attend college? There was also some concern about how my parents and sister would be able to get along on the farm without my help. After some soul searching we decided I must try it.

I talked to a friend who would be a sophomore in Pharmacy the next year. He was in about the same financial situation as I was. We decided to look for a small apartment, batch together and try to find jobs to cover our living costs. There was a college employment office that people contacted if they had odd jobs to be done. We found a cheap apartment that was available in the home of a nice elderly couple some distance from campus.

When it came time for school to start, the son of the teasel owner, who had graduated from Oregon State, arranged for me to stay at his fraternity during Freshman Week to learn the "ins and outs" of college life. This was a good experience but it became obvious I couldn't afford to pledge the fraternity.

My friend and I went ahead with the apartment and batched the first year. It was a good thing I had a Pharmacy major as a roommate because I had never cooked in my life.

When I was in grade school I asked my father "what shall I be when I grow up?" He answered by explaining what people did in different professions and Civil Engineering was one of them which sounded interesting, but it didn't mean much to me then. As years went by I decided it was a profession that made life easier and safer for many people.

I selected Civil Engineering and began my studies. At Molalla I had taken an elective course in trigonometry my senior year and in the placement examinations for college I had been placed in the Math A class starting with calculus. It soon became evident that competition in college was much tougher than high school. Since Oregon State was a Land Grant College at that time all boys had to take a minimum of two years ROTC military training with an option of two more with some pay. There were no girls in my engineering classes and only one in the School of Engineering at that time. She quit after the first semester. My engineering courses were demanding and did not leave much time for elective courses. In my case, there was little time for other activities.

I had contacted the college employment office to see about work and found that it usually consisted of such things as restaurant dishwashing, small house painting jobs, yard work etc. By the time I finished school, I had done all of them. There didn't appear to be any regular jobs available even though the woman who was the longtime manager was very helpful.

After I completed my required surveying classes, my professor who was in charge of the surveying lab, gave me a job adjusting the instruments used by inexperienced students practicing surveying. This practice was done on the lower campus and in a city park with quite a few trees. The college had a truck with an open top with a canvas cover which was used to transport the survey class and equipment. One day I was in the back of the truck with some others and while going through the woods, a limb hit the top and broke a wooden cover support which hit me in the head. This put a gash in my head and required a trip to the hospital. However, it did not turn out to be very serious.

My social life through college was limited. Between working and studying there was little time for the many activities one thinks of as part of college life. I had little contact with girls except staff workers, occasional church attendance, a few dances and required courses for all students. There was little time for athletics although I did some cross country running and some rifle marksmanship in ROTC which helped me later in the Army to become an Expert in all small arms.

My communication with home was limited. Since I had no car at school, the only way to get home was by hitchhiking. I did this occasionally. However, I had been seeing Julia Foglesong, a member of my class in Molalla, during the summer after graduation. She was attending Willamette University and her parents would give me a ride when she was returning to school on the same weekend I was home.

As was fairly common in those times, I sent my dirty clothes by mail in a small cardboard box to my mother. I would always look forward to getting clean clothes and a treat in return.

Where I lived my first year at college did not work out. It was too far from the campus and cooking was a problem. I talked to my friend at the college employment office and she found a job for me closer to campus. The wife of the college president owned a rental duplex which was heated by a sawdust furnace located in the basement where there was also a spare room. If I would take care of the furnace, I could have the room rent free. I took the job and found a boarding house nearby where I had my meals. The next year my friend at the employment office offered me a job to do the same thing at her house. This was even closer to campus and it had a larger room in the basement. I lived there the last two years and took care of her yard and continued to take my meals at the same boarding house.

In 1938 at the end of two years, I had to make the decision whether to stay in ROTC for two more years. I always received good grades in it and I had liked firearms ever since my young friend's grandfather let us play with his 1851 Navy Colt revolver from the Civil War. With the encouragement of the Army Sergeant in charge of the Oregon State program, I signed up. I also appreciated the small amount of pay I received from the program for the next two years.

In 1938 I got a summer job with the Oregon State Highway Department office in McMinnville which covered highways from there to the Oregon Coast. This gave me additional surveying experience on highway rights of way.

As a four year ROTC student at Oregon State I spent the 1939 summer camp at Fort Lewis, Washington. It was a large camp with students from Oregon, Washington and California. We practiced marksmanship, and trench warfare as in World War I. It was a different and interesting experience.

While in college my parents were unable to give me much financial help because of their circumstances. When I got in a real bind I called on Aunt Mabel for a small loan. She was my mother's sister and had been my third grade teacher. I paid these loans back and when I graduated I made the $30 final payment.

During the 1940 academic year I finished all of my requirements for graduation except one course. I was not able to schedule it and had to take it in the summer session. Therefore, I had to wait until Graduation 1941 to receive my degree.

Two years after I left for college, my sister Evelyn graduated from Molalla High School. She went to Linfield and then on to Monmouth. She had a long and successful career as a primary school teacher as well as being a wife and mother of three. We were always very close. She went through college doing housework and babysitting to help pay expenses. Evelyn passed away in 2010.

Several years after I graduated my parents sold the farm and moved back to Willamette. They bought a house next door to the one my grandparents had owned. They lived there until they died; my father in 1948 and my mother in 1960.

Chapter 5

Reflections on My Early Years

When I was a student at Longfellow Jr. High School in Richland, California my English teacher, Miss Cruse, my favorite teacher read "Myself" by Edgar Guest. I thought then it was the best poem I had ever heard. It is still my favorite after all these years. I cannot count the number of times during my life I have remembered the words "I have to live with myself, and so,"

Looking back on my college days, my biggest regret was living alone and having to give so much attention to work and study that it seemed there was little time for anything else. Perhaps because of this, a number of years later I took Dale Carnegie's course "How to Win Friends and Influence People."

Myself

By Edgar Guest

I have to live with myself, and so,
I want to be fit for myself to know;
I want to be able as days go by,
Always to look myself straight in the eye;
I don't want to keep on a closet shelf
A lot of secrets about myself,
And fool myself as I come and go
Into thinking that nobody else will know
The kind of man I really am;
I don't want to dress myself up in sham.
I want to deserve all men's respect;
But here in the struggle for fame and pelf,
I want to be able to like myself.
I don't want to think as I come and go
That I'm for bluster and bluff and empty show.
I never can hide myself from me,
I see what others may never see,
I know what others may never know,
I never can fool myself—and so,
Whatever happens, I want to be
Self-respecting and conscience free.

Chapter 6

Stevens & Koon

In 1920 two highly respected engineers, Jack Stevens and Ray Koon, opened a consulting engineering partnership firm – Stevens & Koon – in Portland, Oregon. World War I was over and the West Coast had been discovered. Oregon and Washington were developing small communities which needed public works. The area was growing - from Portland and Vancouver in the north, to Bend in the east, Coos Bay and beyond in the south and up the Oregon Coast. Water supply and waste treatment, as well as roads and bridges were needed. It was a busy time. During this period Stevens & Koon developed a reputation as a designer of water system development and waste water treatment throughout Oregon and parts of Washington. This included major projects for the City of Portland.

World War II was underway in Europe in 1940 and some felt it was only a matter of time until we would be involved. Perhaps it was time to start some preparations? In 1940 the United States government decided to build the Umatilla Ordnance Depot on a large piece of Government land near Hermiston, Oregon. This was a huge undeveloped tract in sagebrush country populated by Jack Rabbits and Coyotes.

Stevens & Koon designed the project. I had recently completed my requirements for my BS in Civil Engineering from Oregon State and I was looking for a job. My Uncle heard that Stevens & Koon was looking for surveyors to lay out the Umatilla Ordnance Project. One of my professors at Oregon State also suggested this to me. I was very familiar with surveying equipment. As I mentioned, one of my jobs while going to school was working in the lab adjusting equipment after inexperienced students had surveyed parts of the campus. I applied for work at Stevens & Koon and was hired as a rear chainman on a survey crew for $125 a month. This huge tract of land had been previously surveyed and laid out in a grid of 1200 sq. ft. However, the layout for the Ordnance Project was designed for 1000 sq. ft. grid so it needed to be re-surveyed. There were a number of survey crews working on it.

I took a bus to Hermiston one afternoon in the Fall of 1940 and arrived at the hotel that evening. The next morning I found it had snowed during the night – my first view of Hermiston. It was a small town of about 800 people when I arrived and at the height of construction over 7000 workers were involved in the project. I found an upstairs room to rent in the home of a nice elderly couple. I took my meals at a boarding house across the alley. This was my residence for the duration of my job here. While living there I had the opportunity to visit Pendleton and other parts of Eastern Oregon I hadn't seen before.

Our survey crew usually consisted of five men: the Party Chief and Instrument Man, Head Chainman, Rear Chainman, Flag Man, and Station Wagon Driver. The word "chainman" was a carryover from the past. We used 100 foot steel tapes to measure the distance between points. The tape was kept on line by the instrument man. (Today this is all done with digital instruments.) We would drive from Hermiston each morning across the sage brush to the beginning of the day's work. The soil was quite sandy and the wind would form what we called sand blows - piles of sand five or six feet high in places.

One day on the project stands out in my memory. On this particular morning as we arrived at our starting point and I was getting out of the station wagon to get our instruments, I noticed a Coyote duck behind one of the nearby sand blows. We were used to seeing Coyotes and Jack Rabbits but they never came very close. I decided to investigate. I ran to the top of the blow and on the other side was a large Coyote dragging a trap on one hind foot. Not thinking what I would do if I caught him, I yelled to the others and started the chase. The crew jumped in the station wagon and started after us. In spite of the trap, the Coyote could move fairly fast so it took some distance for the crew to catch up with us. One of the crew members jumped out of the wagon and dispatched the Coyote with a steel range pole.

The next thing was what to do with it? The pelt looked good except for the trap mark on the hind foot. We put the Coyote over the front fender of the station wagon and were getting ready to go when the Party Chief, a man of long experience said "Wait fellows, if we take it in like that everyone will think it had a trap on that leg and we just killed it. If someone claimed it was their trap neither of us could probably prove it."

What could we do? He had the answer. I had done some Cross Country running in college and one of the tools we carried on the survey crew was a small hatchet for driving marker stakes. His proposal was that the Coyote had run by me and I had thrown my stake axe, cut him on the hind leg and crippled him so I could run him down and catch him. The word soon got around the project that our crew and I had caught a Coyote.

In the summer the temperature near Hermiston was very warm, sometimes over 100 degrees. We would often stop at a tavern on the way back to town for a beer after work. This was no exception that evening and the Coyote became quite an attraction. I let others tell the story but the pelt was in such a condition that it was hard to prove otherwise. However, I am sure there were some skeptics.

Later the owner of the tavern, who had a number of stuffed animals in the tavern, came to me and said he knew where he could have a nice rug made by a taxidermist for $10.00. I told him I would like that and he brought me a rug with complete pelt, tail, stuffed head, ears, mouth and teeth.

For years this rug rested in our basement playroom and our children referred to it as "goggy". It has now been passed on to grandchildren and enjoyed by great-grandchildren.

Once the property was surveyed and the location of the 1001 concrete igloos, approximately 200 miles of roads and 40 miles of railroad were determined, construction started in earnest. In addition to the igloos there were also conventional buildings constructed. Workmen broke a world record by pouring concrete for twenty-four igloos in twenty-four hours.

The igloos were large buildings for storage of war materials such as ammunition, weapons, bombs, poison gas, etc. They had flat concrete floors and continuous curved walls side to side. They were designed so that if there was an inside explosion, the blast would go up rather than out. They also had to be located a distance apart so an explosion in one could not trigger an explosion in ones next to it.

The Umatilla Ordnance Depot opened in 1941 to prepare for World War II. Since the structures had a fairly low profile, they were not very noticeable from the highway. However, many people in Hermiston did not feel comfortable being so close to a military storage depot. After the war it was not until 1990 that the facility reorganized with complete disposal of war chemicals in October 2011. Some of the igloos are still in use for storage of Red Cross supplies for disaster aid in the Northwest.

As soon as I had saved up some money I bought a 1936 Ford V8 from a farmer. The car was in good condition and lasted until the end of the war. I was then able to drive to Athena, Washington on weekends to see my girl who was teaching High School there. One Sunday I was invited by my boss to bring her to Sunday dinner in Hermiston. I picked her up in Athena and took her to see the project.

When we got there the project was closed up tight because of Pearl Harbor earlier that morning. This reinforced the need for the Ordnance Project.

After a year on the Umatilla project I had learned a lot about surveying and laying out the highway system connecting the igloos. By that time I had advanced considerably in responsibility and was asked to take a position in the Portland office of Stevens & Koon. I was very pleased to be selected to work in the Portland office. After spending so much time on surveying and construction, I was eager to get some design experience on my way to becoming a professional engineer.

About this same time I felt it was time to marry Julia Foglesong. We had attended Molalla High and had our first date on Graduation Night. We continued to see each other during my years at Oregon State and hers at Willamette University as well as during summer vacations and my trips to visit her at Athena. We were married January 25, 1942 at Molalla Methodist Church and took a honeymoon to the Oregon Coast. We rented a small house near Oregon City and I worked at the Stevens & Koon office in the Spalding Building. This was not a large office. It included secretaries, partners, designers and draftsman but resident engineers usually had their offices on projects. I was anxious for the experience but it was not to last.

Having received a ROTC 2nd Lieutenant's Commission in the Army upon graduation from Oregon State, I was called to active duty and reported to Fort Leonard Wood, Missouri for a month long officer refresher course. I was soon on my way to Kansas City on a troop train.

Chapter 7

Fort Leonard Wood & Southern California

Fort Leonard Wood was the home of the 110th Combat Engineer Battalion of the Kansas City National Guard. After a month of experience in military tactics and construction, we received unit assignments. Five of us were assigned to report to the 110th Combat Engineer Battalion at Inglewood, California. We agreed to meet at the Inglewood City Hall on the date at noon with our wives. We did so and found that our Army unit would live in box stalls at Hollywood Race Track and we needed to find quarters for our wives.

My wife and I and another couple, the Roses, were lucky. A doctor who felt sorry for service men offered to rent us a very nice house in Inglewood completely furnished including a grand piano. It was a good place to invite our new Army friends. When the interred Japanese were moved inland, the 110th troops inherited the tar paper shacks they had left at the Santa Anita Race Track. Last stop was Oak Grove Park in Pasadena where the troops lived in Army tents. In the mean time some of our wives had learned what auto camp quarters were like.

During the early part of the war after Pearl Harbor there was considerable concern that the Japanese might attack the California Coast and large aircraft plants. The 110th Combat Engineers were assigned to the Western Defense Command for a short time. As such our job was to patrol parts of Los Angeles at night along the coast looking for submarines. The only suspicious thing I saw which caused some excitement was a fishing boat that slipped anchor. It had a cabin-like conning tower and slowly drifted along the coast. When it landed it was met by a number of our troops.

There were many nice homes on sections of the Los Angeles beaches. Some of these homes belonged to movie stars and they were naturally concerned about them in case of an attack. On our rounds we would check the homes for black-out adequacy and notify owners if there was a problem. Sometimes they would invite us in to see their home so we met quite a few grateful people.

On one occasion there was a bad brush fire near an area of nice homes. We were called upon to help fight this fire giving us that kind of experience also.

After attending camouflage school at March Field, I inspected camouflage at gun emplacements along part of the California coast. These were installed in case of a Japanese attack. Also the roofs of the large aircraft plants in Los Angeles were camouflaged to look like city streets instead of factory buildings.

The Rose Bowl was close to the Oak Grove Park so we got to see the Rose Parade and the last Rose Bowl game before it was moved east during the war. We also enjoyed the sites of Pasadena, Los Angeles, and San Diego. We had the opportunity to spend an unforgettable Thanksgiving at Yellowstone with the Roses. When we received our next assignment our wives left us. Since Julia had given up her teaching job we decided she would live with her parents who owned The Foglesong Feed & Farm Store in Molalla for many years.

The Japanese had taken Attu and Kiska in the Aleutian Islands. Some Alaskans were feeling uneasy. The United States had retaken Attu but with difficulty because of the bad weather and lack of winter equipment. The 110th Combat Engineer Battalion was selected to retake Kiska. After a short period of amphibious war training at Fort Ord, California we left San Francisco in early August 1943 and headed for the Aleutians.

Chapter 8

Kiska

Our ship, the J. Franklin Bell, was one of the older troop ships. It is often rough going out to sea from San Francisco. This was the case and I drew Officer of the Guard the night we left. This meant inspecting the holds of the ship where many of the troops were seasick. I was not a good sailor and after one inspection it was up to the Sergeant of the Guard. We also encountered some bad weather on our way to the Aleutians. We were traveling under blackout conditions at night to avoid Japanese submarines with torpedoes. Information did not travel very fast in those days. Our son Steve was born August 11, 1943 but it was about a month later during the campaign that I got the news via the Red Cross.

The weather in the Aleutians is terrible much of the time and visibility from the air very poor. The plan of attack after studying the maps and doing one practice run on another Alaskan Island was to land on the opposite side of Kiska from the location of the fortification and go across the island to attack. Kiska is a very desolate island, no trees, rough terrain, soft tundra in many places and fierce winds (williwaw) much of the time.

The site for landing had a narrow beach backed by a high steep bank. After much difficulty we got our D-8 Cats to the top of the bank where we used winches on them to unload the ships and pull cargo up the bank. However, it was still necessary to get the weapons, ammunition, etc. across the island. For this we used large Athey Tracked Trailers to cross the tundra.

Living conditions were not good because of the weather. We set up small tents for company functions and a mess hall. Pup tents, sleeping bags, and warm clothing were used for sleeping.

Fortunately, this did not go on for long. When we got to the fortification and harbor on the other side we met no resistance. Apparently, the Japanese had decided that trying to hold Kiska was not worth the effort. Under cover of the weather they had evacuated the garrison by ships and submarines.

However, we had to get all of our material across to the harbor and reload our ships. My platoon was responsible for getting it to the harbor for reloading.

Things hadn't been all bad. There were a number of lakes and a hand grenade in a pond would provide a lot of fish. At one time there had been a fox farm and I saw several Silver Foxes before leaving.

On September 25, 1943 we sailed from Kiska on the USS President Monroe to our next destination – the Hawaiian Islands.

Chapter 9

Oahu

The next stop was Oahu, Hawaii. Our first camp in Oahu was across from Hickam Air Base which had been bombed during the attack on Pearl Harbor, then to Schofield Barracks, and finally a camp near Bellows Airfield on the opposite side of the Island.

Many troops were being sent to Oahu in preparation for duty in the South Pacific. We supervised some of the General Service troops that were constructing barracks and other facilities for arriving troops. The most difficult construction job we had on Oahu was laying an outfall sewer from an Army camp some distance into the Ocean. The problem was not having the right equipment to handle the heavy pipe and get it in place under the water. Fortunately we had some good swimmers. We also attended a school on Jungle Warfare in a location typical of a South Sea Jungle.

It seemed as if the sun was always shining on Hawaii but I was sometimes reminded of Oregon rains when we were having practice drills. There would often be a brief drenching shower that soaked us and then shortly sunshine that would quickly dry us.

I had never been to any of the Hawaiian Islands, so seeing the Memorial at Pearl Harbor, The Royal Hawaiian Hotel (closed to the public and used for military R & R), Diamond Head and the view over the Pali Pass was a great experience for me. I revisited some of these sites several times years later. On a few trips around the island I also enjoyed some of the beaches with giant surf that were frequented by expert surfers.

One of Julia's close sorority sisters at Willamette University was a librarian working in Honolulu. We were able to get together several times while I was there.

While playing tennis on an old concrete court at Schofield Barracks, I had a fall that put me in the large military hospital for a short time. While there I had the opportunity to see Joe Gordon, Johnny Mize and other major league baseball players who entertained the patients in the afternoons. When we had leave we enjoyed the Officer's Club at Waikiki. Earl West, an officer friend, was a distant relative of the Governor. On a few occasions we would visit him at the Governor's mansion. The Governor was an elderly gentleman who liked to play paddle tennis and we would join him on our visits.

Up until then my experience in the Army (with the exception of missing my family) hadn't been too bad. I had been to Alaska, the

Aleutians, and Oahu and seen much. What was next? As combat troops we did not have long to wait.

Chapter 10

Leyte

There had been considerable action in the South Pacific. McArthur had left the Philippines with the vow to return. It appeared the 110th might have the opportunity to assist him. Our first stated objective was the Island of Yap in route to Leyte. However, shortly after leaving Oahu on September 15, 1944 on the USS Alpine the target was changed from Yap to Leyte because a heavy air strike by our Air Force had so damaged Yap. (Several years ago my son and his wife, deep sea divers, visited Yap and saw underwater the results of this bombing.)

The 110th Engineers landed on Violet 2 Beach on October 20, 1944 shortly before McArthur returned. I watched him and his staff wade ashore because the beach was so crowded with boats there was no room for his to land. (I understand the picture was so widely publicized that it was repeated on other landings in the Philippines.) McArthur shortly announced his return to the world.

The war in the South Pacific was somewhat different from that in many other places since so many of the targets were islands that had to be approached across water. The 110th Combat Engineers in addition to conventional military weapons carried heavy construction equipment, trucks, tractors, pile drivers, etc. with which to maintain transportation routes open for supplies and weapons once the troops had landed.

It was not possible to carry this kind of equipment on a regular troop ship. Therefore, the "Landing Ship Tank" nicknamed "LST" was used to transport this type of material to the battle scene across water. This was an ocean going ship on a shallow rounded bottom. Below the main deck was a cargo deck, similar to a car ferry, on which to carry equipment. It had a ramp that lowered on the front end to allow equipment to be discharged. Due to the shallow bottom it could be landed next to a dock or run up on a sandy beach.

The problem with these ships was that they were slow. On an invasion we would have to load them and send them ahead; perhaps with an escort and a few of our men. The majority of the invasion troops would then travel by regular troop ship to rendezvous closer to the landing site. There they would meet and debark to smaller assault boats to land and meet the enemy. Then our LST's would come in and beach to unload.

The landing on Leyte had not been too difficult and we unloaded our heavy equipment quite quickly although a Zero almost got one LST loaded with ammunition while I was on board. We had landed in an undeveloped area and the old country roads and narrow bridges were a continual problem particularly after heavy rains.

I had landed with the 110th but a short time later I was transferred and made Assistant S-3 of Operations for the 24th Engineer Group made up of the 110th, 104th, and 50th Combat Engineers. After being advanced to the rank of Captain I returned to the 110th as Captain of Company A for the rest of the war.

On Leyte during bad weather we sent out bridge guards to watch some of the old narrow bridges. One morning I was flagged down by two guards who said they had been there all night and needed a ride to camp. I told them I would send some relief. Not satisfied, they flagged down another jeep with a driver and an officer who had his cap bill turned up so you could not see his rank. When asked what they wanted, the guards gave the same answer. The officer then asked if he took them who would watch the bridge. The answer "Who the H---- watched it before we came here?" The officer flipped down his cap bill. He was the Commander of the Engineer Group. "Nuf" said.

As I recall we had few problems on Leyte and the Filipinos were quite cooperative. They liked to trade for most anything. A white undershirt got me a nice Bolo knife. I only saw McArthur a couple more times and we continued to train for our next assignment. Shortly before leaving, a large ammunition storage depot near our camp was hit by a night bomber which caused considerable damage.

Chapter 11

Okinawa

Our next stop was Okinawa where we learned what war could be like. We had sailed on the USS Sheridan from Leyte in March 1945. On April 1, 1945 the 110th Engineers landed on Orange 1 Beach, one of several beaches. As we approached the other troop ships and LST's which had preceded us with our heavy equipment, we realized this would be something <u>BIG.</u>

From the time we had loaded the Higgins landing craft from the ship and headed for the beach we saw a fireworks show like none I had seen before or since. The sky seemed full of Japanese Zero's and from the sea our battle ships were firing at the planes leaving fiery trails that would crash in the water. We were perhaps about the 5th wave and there was not much enemy resistance except for some low flying Zeros. On Orange 1 we immediately began to unload our equipment from the LST's so they could get off the beach and not become bomber targets. The land appeared to slope up from the beaches so the Japanese had apparently moved inland to higher ground and were waiting for us there.

We set up our camp inland in a canyon where we were better protected from artillery fire. There was a battery of our 150mm cannons some distance to the rear and another Japanese battery to the front. At night they would duel. Every time a 150 mm shell went over our heads it sounded like a freight train. The Japanese response was to return fire in increments with each getting closer to us. We slept in tents but had foxholes close by and we could tell by the sound when it was time to go for one.

Construction and maintenance of roads and bridges was our responsibility. Again there were many narrow old roads and weak bridges. Also there were heavy rains at times and low lying areas. We opened a quarry but the coral material was very soft when it got wet. A section of road might look nice at day's end but like mush after a hard rain during the night.

Bridges were another problem. There was an old wooden bridge over a ravine about 150 feet deep supported by wood pilings that needed reinforcing and a new deck. I received an emergency request that a company of tanks was moving in and needed to use this bridge to cross over the ravine. We set up a temporary camp beside the bridge, scavenged the area and found some lumber to re-deck it. We worked all night and the tanks were about due. I sent the men back to camp for breakfast. I was still somewhat worried about the bridge support so I decided to take another look down below. I planned to ask the tank commander to go very slow across the bridge. As I got to the bottom of the gulley I heard the tanks coming and they didn't sound slow. By the time I got to the top the first tank, without slowing down, made it across as did the rest. I don't remember ever feeling more relief.

We often worked on roads at night and sometimes Japanese bombers would be in our area. We had a "red alert" system for truck drivers to blackout when this happened. Apparently late one night a driver didn't get the word and led bombers to our motor pool. They caused much damage to the motor pool and killed the driver. They also dropped a string of "time release" bombs on the camp. The next morning while the men were lined up at the mess tent two of these went off causing casualties.

As I mentioned earlier, much of the soil was quite soft so we checked the camp for entry sites of more bombs. One of my sergeants and I had both been to demolition school and knew the way to detonate them was to shape powder charges over the entry holes. We tried this and succeeded only in the shape charges blowing holes in our tents. I decided we would have to move the camp farther down the canyon which we did. About 2:00 A.M. the next morning more bombs went off.

As the war moved inland there was disruption of the civilian population. There were quite a few caves and we would encounter people hidden in them. Near the end there was quite a large number located in a steep cliff along the ocean beach. The 110th Company A was asked to remove them. This was not an easy task because the bank was steep and some of the caves were small and others quite large. Also, the occupants were frightened that they would be harmed if they surrendered. My First Sergeant and I were checking out the site when he went to the bottom of the cliff and looked in a small cave. Just inside he saw a Samurai sword which indicated a Japanese officer might be present. Suddenly there was movement and my Sergeant lost no time getting out. We waited nearby and shortly heard a hand grenade go off inside.

The officer had committed suicide rather than surrender. Samurai swords were well crafted, often highly valued and handed down in families. I kept the sword for a number of years as a war souvenir until I met a collector who said he might be interested in locating the family. I don't know if he ever did, but his last report was that he had determined that the blade had been slightly shortened indicating it had been altered for a shorter person than the original owner.

I felt sorry for these frightened people some of whom would rather die than give up. Some were reported to have jumped off cliffs. Okinawa took the lives of 12,281 Americans and 110,071 Japanese soldiers.

After the battle at Okinawa was over we were told that our next stop was Japan. We were to get our equipment in first class condition for this next move. It did not take us long to do this. We had all the equipment lined up and it was ready to go.

Then one morning I went down to mess and heard that an atomic bomb had been dropped over Hiroshima, Japan followed shortly by another over Nagasaki.

The next thing we knew the war was over. I had over 100 points so I would be going home. The 110th Engineering Combat Battalion would be going on to Korea instead of Japan.

On October 16, 1945 I sailed from Okinawa on the USS Botetourt. On October 31, 1945 I debarked in San Francisco. After separation at Fort Lewis, Washington I returned to Oregon City by train and met my 27 month old son for the first time. His first words – "Can we have a puppy now?" That Christmas he received a little black Cocker Spaniel named Inky.

Chapter 12

Reflections on the War Years

In conclusion of this period of my life of about 4 ½ years in the US Army as an Engineer officer, I cannot say enough good things about the men I served with. I gave many of them orders they may have not liked but I can truthfully say I only seriously considered requesting Court Marshal for one. As a company commander one of the toughest things for me was writing a letter of condolence to the wife of one of my men.

There were difficult times, but I learned a lot about leadership and how to take the initiative and get things done when dealing with men. Although most of us spent only a short time in the Army, it is surprising the strength of the bond between soldiers who have served in combat together. In the beginning of the war most members of the 110th Combat Engineer Battalion were from the Kansas City area and part of the National Guard. By the end of the war due to replacements for various reasons we had representatives from many states. The bonds between these men were strong. Each year a national reunion of the 110th was held at a different location for the convenience of members in the U.S. We held these reunions for 30 years until our ranks became so small it was no longer practical. I still get a few Christmas cards.

I believe this bond can be better understood by this eulogy presented by Ed Lindsay, a Sergeant in Company A, at a memorial for one of our members.

A BUDDY

A person's life is enriched by many associations – his Mom, his Dad, his first Girlfriend, his Wife, his Children, his Grandchildren. . . These are all important to him.

Yet, there is another special association that not all men can have, but those who do are indeed fortunate. He can have friends—but only in the human emotion of military service can he have a "Buddy". Many men have several "Buddies", but the one most important of all is that special Buddy.

The military experience forges many alliances – duty, honor, country. The ties are strong when fused by the heat of battle, but none are fused more closely than those with your Buddy. He is your mental and moral strength for all experiences, his sounding board for all victories and defeats; someone who thinks like he does, who can relate to what he feels.

That is what a Buddy is. . . Sometimes we lose our Buddy. Sometimes it is in battle and sometimes it happens later in years.

Nothing changes, however, whether your Buddy is yet alive or has passed on. It does not ever change. He will be your Buddy forever. The tie never is broken, and this is one of life's rewards. . . you cannot lose a Buddy. He is in your memory forever.

May God bless and keep my Buddy and may he rest in the grace of the Lord eternally.

Ed Lindsey

Chapter 13

Back to Work

I was now faced with a new and different set of circumstances. After a reunion with my family it was necessary to find work and a place to live with them. I went to the Stevens & Koon office in Portland where I was well received and offered a position at a better salary than I had before leaving.

Finding a place to live was a more difficult story. There had been many new houses built in the Portland area while I was gone. We looked at a number of them and saw some we liked but they cost about $15,000. Since Julia and Steve had lived with her parents while I was gone, I had invested most of my officer's pay in War Bonds but only had about $4000 in savings. I knew these $15,000 houses had cost about half that to build before the war and thought the prices would come down. I was reluctant to take on so much debt. We continued to look and after much thought settled for a small, older, one bedroom house in a good location at 5713 SE 41st Avenue in Portland. It was December 5, 1945 and we paid $4000. My daughter Nancy was born on August 23, 1946. We lived in this house with its crowded conditions for about six years.

In January 1946 I went back to work at Stevens & Koon. There were quite a few changes in the office. Portland had been a busy place during the War with many people arriving to work at the Kaiser Shipyards. The city had grown and there was demand for larger and additional sanitary facilities. Stevens & Koon and John W. Cunningham & Associates had a joint venture to draw plans for major sewage projects that would be able to be built after the War.

With so many engineers in the service during the War there were some shortages. During the summers, Stevens & Koon brought a young professor, Loren Thompson, from Rose-Hulman Institute of Technology out to Portland to assist them. Subsequently he became a Junior Partner. I had been called into the Army before I had an opportunity to add much to my college training in design. At Stevens & Koon I now had the chance to work beside experts and they were most helpful. I also needed this kind of experience so I could take the exams for registration as a Professional Engineer in the different states. Between on the job experience and studying at home in the evenings, I was able to become registered in Oregon, Washington, Idaho and Alaska as a Professional Engineer.

Between 1946 and 1949 I gained considerable experience on a variety of projects. Loren and I had designed a secondary sewage treatment plant for Chehalis, Washington. When the design was bid, it was decided it would be a good idea for me to be Resident Engineer on the project. This would give me construction experience on a project I had designed. This presented a good opportunity but also a problem. With a wife and two children and having just purchased our first home in Portland, a job in Chehalis, Washington did not sound too attractive. However, after careful consideration, the opportunity won out.

The solution was for me to drive to Chehalis on Sunday evenings and return home to Portland on Friday evenings, a distance of about 100 miles each way. I stayed at the St. Helens Hotel during the week for the duration of the project. I had to be sure to bring home a little gift each Friday. I have often felt sorry for those times when Julia was left alone with the children during the week. I learned a lot and had an opportunity to see how well things went together that I had designed, but this was my first and last Resident Engineer job.

The project was very important for Chehalis. It was a brand new plant with all the features of both a primary and secondary plant. Things went well with the construction and the contractor was very competent and cooperative.

About noon one day I noticed the power poles and wires in the street shaking as the result of a fairly strong earthquake. This caused some concern because the day before we had poured the concrete for a large digester tank. When I went back to my hotel that evening I found a large crack between the wall and the ceiling. Fortunately there was no damage done at the plant.

The Chehalis representatives took a lot of interest in the project. The Mayor visited on a regular basis and I would show him around the job site and explain what we were doing. When the project was finished and the bronze plaque was put on the control building I was surprised to see my name as Resident Engineer listed along with the other dignitaries. I had never seen that done before and when I thanked the Mayor, he said I deserved it. I felt very good about it because I had lived with the project from beginning to end. I had learned a lot from my first significant design job. At that time I had no idea how many more were to come.

When I was released from the Army I had elected to stay in the Reserve. I was assigned to a Boat & Shore Battalion that met at Vancouver Barracks for meetings. This was no problem while I was working in Portland. However, Chehalis was another story so I had resigned my commission while working there. About a month later I got word my unit had been sent to Korea. I felt very fortunate and sorry for those who had to go again.

Chapter 14

Stevens, Thompson & Runyan

In 1951, after 31 years, Ray Koon decided to retire from Stevens & Koon. An interesting note is that he had attended Stanford and was an Engineering classmate of Herbert Hoover in 1893. At the time Ray Koon retired, I was made an Associate of the firm along with long time employee Frank Kohler. This did not mean we had ownership but rather a share of the profits if there were any. During the next five years the backlog of necessary public works after the War kept us pretty busy and I had the opportunity to get more experience and responsibility.

The year 1951 also made a change in our family living conditions. We had been looking for a larger house and decided to find a lot and have one built to our plan. Accordingly, we bought a ½ acre lot, hired a contractor and our house was built at 16116 SE River Road near Oak Grove, Oregon.

This area at the time was in the process of development and there was convenient transportation to my office in Portland. We were able to have a large yard and garden. It was a comfortable house but initially had one problem. There was no sanitary sewer system in the area at the time only septic tanks. During high rainfall periods we would get some water in the basement. This required a sump pump until several years later our firm designed the sanitary sewer system and treatment plant for the Sanitary Districts No. 1 and No. 2 in the area. During the construction I found it a bit difficult to live in the area. If the contractor did something my neighbors didn't like, I would hear about it.

Steve and Nancy attended Concord Elementary School and Milwaukie High School. Julia was active in the Oak Grove Garden Club and a past president. We attended the Oak Grove Methodist Church. The little black Cocker Spaniel, Inky, that Steve received after I returned from the war had been killed by an auto. She was replaced with Pat, a terrier, who lived for 13 years.

This was a growing area and we found it a pleasant place to live. It was close enough for Steve and Nancy to see their grandparents frequently as well as aunts, uncles and cousins. The children did well in their schoolwork and participated in other activities. Steve was an Eagle Scout and a member of the wrestling team and Nancy was on the rally squad. This is where we lived until they went to college, Steve to Stanford and Nancy to Oregon State.

They are both now retired, Steve as CEO of his company and Nancy as Vice-President where she worked.

In 1954 Jack Stevens decided to retire. At that time Loren Thompson and I were offered an opportunity to acquire the firm for what we considered to be a favorable price considering its prospects and reputation. I was able to pay my share by a loan from my father-in-law. The name became Stevens, Thompson & Runyan. We retained Stevens' name partly for appreciation as well as for his stature in the profession. At that time, the names of prominent founders were often retained and if the names became too long then just the initials were used. For example, we were often referred to as STR and we designed a corresponding logo. Stevens had been national president of the American Society of Civil Engineers in 1944-1945. He was the inventor of a remote recorder to measure stream flow as well as being a consultant on Bonneville Dam, a well known landmark, and other large projects. Loren and I were both active in the practice and the profession by this time.

It was decided that the firm would be a partnership with the two of us as partners. Loren, the older and more experienced, was President and I was Executive Vice President. Recognizing the different priorities in a consulting business, we both wished to be as much involved in all phases – Development, Design, and Management – as practical. I feel that throughout our partnership we balanced our responsibilities to maximize our individual capabilities. We adopted a practice of assigning responsibility to a Partner for each major project. In most instances if it was Clean Water, Loren would have responsibility and if it was Waste Water, it would be mine. I sometimes felt I got to clean up the mess.

From 1950-1955 due to backlogs of work to be done following the end of the War, we were kept busy and the firm became larger and more diversified.

When I was in college there were about five different classifications of engineers: Civil, Electrical, Mechanical, Structural, and Mining. After the War many more were added. There were no large multi-discipline engineering firms located in Portland. If you were a consultant in an engineering specialty and needed help in another field you would have to go to another consultant for help. Under the partner system Stevens & Koon operated pretty much like a Doctor's office. Each partner had his regular clients and used other members of the staff to assist in accomplishing the work as well as going outside to get special help. This meant additional agreements, less control and sometimes delays. We realized the development of a multi-discipline office would take time but was indeed a worthy goal. Going forward we kept this objective in mind as we selected our staff.

During the period 1955-1960 Stevens, Thompson & Runyan continued to grow. We added additional engineering, architectural and planning personnel acquainted with the fields of private, municipal and governmental design and construction. In 1959 offices were established in Seattle, Washington and Boise, Idaho. One in Spokane, Washington was opened later. We became not only a multiple office company but also a multi-discipline firm.

After the War during the Red Scare in Alaska we were asked by our government to design improvements to the underground facilities of their Alaska Airbases. We opened joint venture offices in Fairbanks and Anchorage through which we designed water and sewage treatment facilities for these cities also.

In the early years the firm's office was on the 10th floor of the Spalding Building in downtown Portland. It was at that location when I was hired before World War II. This was a convenient location but the offices were small and not designed for drafting room space or growth in staff.

Shortly after I returned to the Portland office after the War, the firm moved to the 2nd floor of the National Building. It provided better working space but soon became crowded. Parking for our employees was a problem and there was no space for a break or lunch room. However, there was one feature enjoyed by both employees and their families. We were on the Rose Festival parade route and we had excellent viewing from our second floor location.

We were quite conscious of the importance of working conditions for our staff and decided to look for another space. At that time there was a large urban renewal project about to get underway in Southwest Portland. We considered the possibility of designing a building and having it built to our specifications. We found a lot adjacent to the boundary of the urban renewal site which met our needs. We designed a two story building with office and drafting space on the upper floor. There was a lunch and break room as well as future space on the lower floor. Fortunately our building was finished about the time the urban renewal project got started and the City Staff for the project rented part of our lower floor for a period of time.

In 1961 we formed the corporation, Stevens, Thompson & Runyan, Inc. Historically major decisions had been made by the two partners. However, after incorporation our Board of Directors included President Loren Thompson, Executive Vice President & Treasurer Marvin Runyan, Vice Presidents James Crom, Gilbert Meigs, Wilfred Amble and Harold Murray, plus outside members Carl Hopp and E. Robert de Luccia.

From the beginning of STR we developed very detailed Personnel Handbooks for our employees stating our policies and expectations of them as well as what they could expect from STR.

As our staff and client list grew we began publishing our monthly newsletter "INTERCOM". This was distributed in each of our offices and contained articles about current projects as well as updates on staff members and new additions to our team.

Our quarterly publication "STRIDES" was sent to clients and suppliers to keep them aware of our activities and the capabilities of our staff for future projects. There was some surprise when we first announced the addition of architecture to our practice. However, it was not our intent to provide this service other than on our own projects.

We encouraged our staff to be active in professional activities. A number of our young engineers became officers in professional societies and later some branched out and started their own firms.

In the early years the Portland office had an annual picnic at Blue Lake Park. We always valued our staff highly because they made the firm what it was.

Due to the STR workload I began to find that time for vacations of any length were difficult. The family enjoyed the beaches at the Oregon Coast and for several summers we spent vacations there that were all too short. At that time we couldn't justify owning a cabin for the amount of time we were spending there.

In the summer of 1966 after an especially nice vacation at Lincoln City we started looking at property and you guessed it – we bought an older house on the ocean front at Lincoln City at 3529 N. Jetty Ave. We enjoyed time there for a number of years for ourselves and other family members.

The 1960's and 1970's were busy times for the firm. It seemed that the rest of the country had realized things were happening in the Pacific Northwest and Alaska. After the War one of my college professors and four of his former students formed CH2M Hill and became our strongest competitor and also a fine multi discipline firm.

In 1974 I was very pleased to be selected Outstanding Civil Engineer of the Year by the Oregon Section of the American Society of Civil Engineers (ASCE). Loren had received this honor in 1958.

During Loren and my partnership we had divided up responsibilities. Portland was always our headquarter office and it was my responsibility. Loren was the one to develop branch offices and their operations. Water was one of the primary commodities with which we were involved. Loren was more experienced in fresh water treatment and my specialization was waste water disposal. Therefore, Loren was more inclined to the dams and filter plants and I to waste water plants and sewage disposal systems. Interaction of disciplines was a key to STR's project management. A number of engineers, planners and architects may provide input to achieve the most comprehensive solution for an assignment. This team approach requires careful coordination by a project manager and the officer of the firm responsible for the project. With this approach the client has direct contact with both the officer and the project manager. To augment our expertise we depended on the multi-discipline capacity of the firm's civil, electrical, mechanical, structural, architectural, and planning staff to get the job done.

During the growth years some of the larger projects included those for the City of Portland. Bull Run Dam No.2 was an important element in the water storage and supply system for Portland. Other major projects for the City of Portland included the 100 million per day secondary treatment facilities at the Columbia Boulevard wastewater treatment plant and many sewage pumping stations. For Washington County, the Durham Advanced Tertiary Waste Water Facility with an initial capacity of 20 million gallons per day and expandable to 60 million gallons per day by 1980 was a key project. In addition to all three neighboring counties in the Portland metropolitan area, many smaller water and waste water facilities had been designed. This extended to other parts of Oregon, Washington, Idaho, Alaska and beyond. Other types of public works such as roads, bridges, power houses and sub-stations as well as city planning were included. STR had become a multi discipline firm.

About this time we faced another office problem. The Oregon State Highway Department had a route change for a major highway and wanted to include the STR building site in it. We had little choice. Loren and I had financed the building and charged STR rent for the space at what we considered a reasonable rate. We decided to see if we could find a replacement location. This resulted in our finding a one block lot at 5505 S.E. Milwaukie Avenue, Portland, Oregon. We designed and eventually built two buildings on this site and acquired parking space across the street. These buildings served us very well and provided some rental space to others.

Other large engineering firms in different areas of the country were forming large conglomerates by buying smaller firms in developing areas of the country. Some of these conglomerates were on the American Stock Exchange.

Suddenly three large firms all at one time indicated interest in purchasing Stevens, Thompson & Runyan. We had never given any indication of interest in such, but agreed to give it some thought. When we started to diversify and expand our in-house capabilities we had adopted a policy that in addition to bonuses at the end of the year we would distribute some stock in the company to selected office and section managers. A number of employees had been receiving this stock but up till then no market existed for it. Some of them had growing families thinking about college. Loren and I had retained the stock majority and had no particular interest in selling but thought in the interest of what was then a total of 18 stockholders it was worth investigating.

We interviewed the three different companies and then received proposals from each. After review by the stockholders we voted on June 15, 1973. The winner was CRS Design Associates, Inc.; at that time one of the largest architectural engineering companies in the U.S. They were listed on the American Stock Exchange and their main office was located in Houston, Texas. The terms of the sale made it possible for Stevens, Thompson & Runyan stockholders to receive part of their money without delay. The name of the firm remained the same, Stevens, Thompson & Runyan, Inc. but being part of a public company on the stock exchange made some changes. The transition went quite smoothly. Further expansion of the firm followed and it soon had offices in Houston, Phoenix and Los Angeles. This was followed by a large water project in Milwaukee, Wisconsin.

During these years not very many U.S. engineering firms had offices overseas as is quite common today. CRS Design Associates had a military academy design project in Saudi Arabia which our Houston office was involved with. They also had an office in London and considered locations in other countries.

In 1976 Loren retired after 30 years with the firm and I became President and Chairman of Stevens Thompson & Runyan. He left a very impressive record of service to the profession and those of us who worked with him. He and I always had a fine working relationship. We didn't always at first agree but I cannot remember a time we didn't amicably resolve a problem. I guess I must have begun to realize how some of the previous partners felt when one would retire. Suddenly I realized that I too had been around a long time and began to look at 1980 as a target date for retirement. By this time we had a number of capable office managers so I had no concerns about the future of STR.

Since our merger in 1973 with CRS Design Associates (CRSDA) they had continued to acquire additional firms. One of them was A.A. Mathews (AAM) which was internationally acclaimed for its reputation in underground engineering and construction management. Their headquarters was in Rockville, Maryland and they also had offices in New York and Los Angeles where they did subway work. Since the work they did was somewhat special and closer to what Stevens, Thompson & Runyan (STR) was doing than any other CRSDA companies, it was decided it would make sense to merge the two. Accordingly that was done and the name was changed to STRAAM.

I became CEO of STRAAM in 1978 and found myself responsible for 10 offices and 250 employees scattered all over the U.S. and Alaska. These offices were located in Portland, Oregon; Seattle, Washington; Boise, Idaho; Los Angeles, California; Houston, Texas; Phoenix, Arizona; Milwaukee, Wisconsin; Atlanta, Georgia; New York City, New York; Rockville, Maryland; as well as joint venture offices in Anchorage and Fairbanks, Alaska.

Up until then I had little time to travel and do other things. I enjoyed the overseas travel I experienced in the Army, but realized there was much more to be seen than the South Pacific Islands and the

Aleutians. Vacations, professional organization meetings, and business travel had given me the opportunity to see much of the United States, but little beyond. In addition I felt my wife was entitled to some of these benefits.

Accordingly, I made plans to retire by the end of 1979 after 39 years with the firm. This would give other deserving staff an opportunity for promotion and to implement any necessary reorganization between CRSDA and STRAMM. By then I would be 61 years old which seemed time for a change and a chance to give others the kind of opportunity I had enjoyed.

During those 39 years there were numerous projects I was involved with as responsible officer-in-charge. Many of these were water and sewage projects including master planning, financial and organizational analysis, water quality studies, engineering design, and construction. Some of these were located in Portland, Milwaukie, Durham, Hillsboro, Dallas, Coos Bay, North Bend, Lincoln city, and Taft in the state of Oregon. In Washington State, there were projects in Vancouver, Longview, Winlock, Chehalis, Aberdeen, and Walla Walla. Also included in some were sewage pumping and collection systems for local service districts within the cities. Over these years I have seen the processes of water and waste water treatment develop from primary to secondary to tertiary including industrial wastes and producing effluent ready for re-use. I believe these projects qualify as having made life better and safer for many people.

Throughout my career I was always active in professional affairs. I am a Fellow and Life Member of the Oregon Section of the

American Society of Civil Engineers (ASCE) and in addition to other major committee assignments was chairman of a national committee which developed a new Code of Ethics for ASCE. I also served as president of the Consulting Engineers Council of Oregon, the Engineers and Architects Council of Oregon, and the Pacific Northwest Pollution Control Association. Other professional activities include National Society of Professional Engineers (NSPE), American Water Works Assoc. (AWWA), American Public Works Assoc. (APWA), diplomat and Trustee-at-Large of the American Academy of Environmental Engineers all of which have awarded me Life Membership. I have received the Bedell Award of the Water Pollution Control Federation, and the Outstanding Civil Engineer Award of the Oregon Section of ASCE. A long time member of Rotary Club of Portland, I am a Paul Harris Fellow.

On June 30, 1979 STRAAM celebrated its first birthday. I had previously advised the president of CRSDA and members of the STR board of my desire to retire at that time. The announcement to the staff in general was met by surprise. However, I was also able to report a profitable year for STRAAM along with appropriate salary adjustments for the next fiscal year.

My retirement was effective July 1, 1979. I was asked by the CRS Group to remain until a new president was selected and to be available for future assignments during the transition. This was not yet the end of expansion. In 1984 STRAAM expanded again to better serve local pulp and paper companies. In 1989 the Portland office designed and built a wafer fabrication facility in Gresham, Oregon.

By 1994 when Jacobs Engineering, a large international engineering company, acquired the company, the Portland office was well established in the conductor industry and was one of the Northwest's leading pulp and paper consultants.

Chapter 15

Reflections on My Career

I selected Civil Engineering when I went to Oregon State because something my Father told me years before had interested me. This led to the realization that design of public works could make life easier and better for many.

Both Jack Stevens and Ray Koon (founders of Stevens & Koon) and Loren Thompson were fine gentlemen and excellent engineers. I have always considered myself fortunate to receive my first job from them as soon as I finished my education at Oregon State. My first assignment led to surveying and construction experience but was interrupted by the war. However, it was great to return to the firm after the war and continue my quest to become a Registered Professional Civil Engineer. They supported me all the way.

As I now look back I am reminded of the roles other individuals and groups have had in my career. I have avoided mentioning individuals because there are so many of them. The foundation I received from my teachers and mentors along the way made it possible.

FAMILIES: For the members of my family I haven't the words to express my gratitude. Likewise, this applies to the STR family that supported me for so many years. I deeply appreciate the efforts of this dedicated staff resulting in the success of our many projects. I have sometimes received more credit for this cooperative effort than I deserved. I am still often reminded of the fine STR employees of the past. I recently attended the Memorial Service for one of our women employees who was 102.

CITY COUNCILS: When I began attending City Council meetings to discuss their problems I discovered they had given a lot of thought to possible solutions. Once a plan was agreed on they would make the effort to raise the necessary funds to do the job. This usually took a lot of meetings and many hours of work to accomplish. I always appreciated the efforts of these public servants and staff involved.

EQUIPMENT MANUFACTURER'S REPS: As designers of facilities requiring quite complicated machinery we needed an assurance before specifying and recommending equipment to our clients. In this regard I appreciated the time and quality of information provided to us by many fine representatives of the manufacturers.

CONTRACTORS: Perhaps the most important is the final result. I have appreciated the many fine contractors who built the structures and installed the equipment in accordance with our plans and specifications. Result, to my knowledge, only one construction accident with a loss of life on one of our hundreds of projects.

PROFESSIONAL ORGANIZATIONS: Civil Engineering is a pretty demanding course in college and having worked my way through school, I had little time for non-required electives. As a result I was exposed to very few business related courses.

During the early years of becoming an owner and manager I found the American Society of Civil Engineers (dating back to my student chapter days at Oregon State) and other related technical and professional societies plus Downtown Portland Rotary Club very valuable to me as a source of continuing education. Rotary was refreshing to me for over 40 years because it made it possible for me to meet with business men and women and discuss matters other than engineering on a regular basis.

Active participation in these societies at both the local and national level gave me a great deal of information on the technical side as well as management of a business. The culmination was the opportunity to be National Chairman of the American Society of Civil Engineers New Code of Ethics Committee. This was a five year effort with cooperation by other engineering societies to develop a standard code of ethics for the engineering profession. Up until its adoption most engineering organizations had covered a number of common items but there were some variations and no standard. It has been felt this was a valuable contribution to the profession for which I am proud. The revised code, adopted by the ASCE Board of Directors in

September 1976, comprises four fundamental principles, seven fundamental canons, and the guidelines to practice.

THE CHURCH: My parents were married in the Willamette Methodist Church on June 18, 1916 and were long time members of the church. I went to Sunday school regularly when I was a boy and have been a member of the Oak Grove Methodist Church since 1955. I can still remember some outstanding Sunday school teachers and one in particular who took us on week-end outings. I have a very high regard for the church experiences I have had throughout my life.

Chapter 16

Retirement

The afternoon of June 21, 1979 a large reception was held at the STRAAM Portland office to celebrate my 39 years of service. Portland Mayor Frank Ivancie and many of our clients, friends and Portland staff were present. It was a great send off after receiving considerable press about the STRAAM merger and my retirement.

For a time during retirement I was available for special assignments for the firm, and served on professional and Rotary committees. As a retirement gift, STRAAM gave us a trip to London which we extended to include Scotland, Ireland and the rest of England. This was the beginning of "catching up" on vacation time. We subsequently traveled to Norway, Sweden, Denmark, and Australia as well as US cities and national parks, and attended several Army reunions. I was able to continue my hobbies of photography, and antique Colt Firearms collecting plus my boyhood interest in automobiles.

I belonged to the Oregon Arms Collectors and went to local gun shows as well as traveling to Las Vegas several times a year to attend international gun shows. There I met collectors and dealers from all over the world. As a result in a period of 25 years between 1969, when I obtained an 1851 Colt revolver like the one my little friend and I played with so many years ago, and 1994 I collected over 100 Colt revolvers of different models. I took pictures of my guns to document my collection and as my collection grew so did my interest in photography. In order to downsize, on May 30-31, 1994 I placed a large part of my collection in an auction at Butterfield & Butterfield in San Francisco. (Goodbye gun collecting).

Ever since that first 1927 Chevrolet, I have been interested in automobiles. Originally we were a one car family but soon became a two car family. We had many cars over the years and one was usually a sports car which I drove. However, I usually drove a company car on business calls. Although I owned a number of different ones over the years, Porsche was always my favorite. I sold my last sports car, a red 1990 Miata MX5, when I was 92. (Goodbye sports cars).

After retirement we continued to live in our home in Dunthorpe, adjacent to Lake Oswego, Oregon. Purchased in 1969, it was our dream home. Located on a one acre site, half of the property was a natural setting with large fir trees like the ones at the home where I was born, and the other half was landscaped. The large yard kept me busy part of the time. We made frequent visits to our vacation home in Coronado Shores on the Central Oregon Coast which we purchased in 1982. We loved our homes and between them, travel, friends and family we had a wonderful life for many years. Unfortunately along the way Julia developed heart problems resulting in surgery and was later diagnosed with Parkinson's disease which affected her mobility. In the 1990's this became more severe and we decided it would be best to move to a place where she could receive better care as needed.

When we moved to Willamette View retirement home in 1996 it was sort of like moving back home. Willamette View at 12705 S.E. River Road is only a short distance north of the house we had built 45 years ago on River Road.

In the 50's the first building of the Willamette View complex was an eight story rectangular concrete building in a large open field. When Julia and I used to drive by we would say "Boy, I would never live in a place like that with all those old people".

Many things change and so had we and Willamette View. When we moved in it had developed into a group of well designed buildings with beautifully landscaped and maintained grounds and about 500 of those old people. We didn't call them old people any longer because now they were our friends and neighbors. (One of my close neighbors today is an active 103 year old woman). Before I sold the Miata I had magnetic signs made which I stuck on the sides of the car and we would drive in local parades with the top down: "Willamette View – Where the Old Stay Young."

On February 21, 1998 my family hosted a luncheon at Atwater's in Portland to celebrate my 80th birthday. In addition to our children and grandchildren, it was attended by over 50 relatives and dear friends. The weather was nice, the view of the city was spectacular and the food was great. It was one of the last memorable events Julia and I were able to attend.

Julia passed away on June 18, 2000. I am very thankful we were able to spend her last four years together at Willamette View.

I continue to live in our beautiful apartment which overlooks the Willamette River and surrounding area. Not only is there fine care available here, but there are many activities which I enjoy photographing for the monthly "Willamette Views" publication. I still enjoy trips to the beach and during the past 10 years have been able to continue my travels to faraway places with members of my family. I have visited Europe (2001), New Zealand (2002), China (2003), Russia (2004), Africa (2005), Alaska (2006), Greece (2007), Danube River (2008), Northwest Passage (2009) and Victoria B.C. (2010).

Chapter 17

Travel

Travel has been a very important part of my life and I have seen great changes over time. During my many years of travel, I have covered thousands of miles over land, air and water.

Previously I referred to my interest in the automobile. I can still clearly remember the Model T Ford with a brass radiator and crank starter that belonged to my step-grandfather.

I am most thankful that I have never had a serious injury during my travels although I had a memorable accident while driving from California to Portland. Julia and I were returning from a Christmas visit with the family. Steve and Jan were driving back with us and we took turns driving. When it was my turn to drive the conditions were dry but there was a little snow along the edges of the highway. I was traveling at the speed limit when we reached a hill at the beginning of the Siskiyou Mountains. I did not make a speed adjustment because there did not seem to be a change in the road condition. When we got about three-fourths of the way up the hill I noticed a car off to the right side of the road. At the same time my car felt like it was on air, steering was unresponsive and the car slid in a circle to the right where it ended up against a steeply cut bank. We were badly shaken but unhurt. The car was a total wreck. The important part of the story is that if the car had spun out to the left side – there was a 200 foot drop-off.

The driver of the car I had noticed on the side of the road had called Highway Patrol when he spun out. When they arrived they told us everything had been fine until 4:00 p.m. when the temperatures dropped. I had hit black ice. There have not been any other accidents but I have to admit to two speeding tickets.

I have not traveled a great deal by railroad. I do remember some beautiful sights from rail cars but they passed quickly. Perhaps the most memorable train rides were from Portland to Walla Walla. We had several projects in Walla Walla, Washington which was quite a drive from Portland. On some inspection trips I would get on the train in the evening in Portland and be in Walla Walla for breakfast. The problem was in between since this was a "milk run" and the train stopped at every small town along the way. It would set me up in my berth each time it jolted to a stop both going and coming back.

My memory of airplanes goes back to when I was a small boy going to the County Fair where there would be a pilot and a small bi-plane offering to take you up for an hour for a few bucks.

One of the largest airplanes I remember seeing was a B-29 on Leyte. Someone saw it land on the airfield, passed the word and I went to see it. It was necessary to climb a ladder to get inside.

During the war the Japanese had the Baka Bomb which would literally be flown by the pilot directly into the target. There was also the Japanese Zero which was an exceptional plane but we liked to see our fighter planes much better.

In later years more of my travel was done by air. Early on I would sometimes fly along the Oregon Coast on a small airline that would make quite a few stops at small towns. They would often just shut down one engine on a twin engine plane long enough to allow passengers to get off or on that side of the plane.

On a flight from the Chicago area on a twin jet, one of the engines stopped during take-off. Fortunately, the pilot was able to stop the plane before we reached the end of the runway.

I used to fly on DC-8's on my first flights to Fairbanks. They were quite slow and noisy. I always remember the first flight on a jet to Alaska. It was a beautiful, clear day and all the way from our high elevation I could see the Alaska Highway winding below us.

I have had quite a few long walks and waits in modern airports and been in lots of traffic jams, but usually got to my destination on time. I have had luggage arrive late, but I have never lost any luggage.

My memory of water travel goes back to rowboats, canoes and paddle wheel ferry boats followed by troop ships, Higgins boats and cruise ships.

While in the Army I traveled on a number of different troop ships. I have mentioned before that I was not a very good sailor in bad weather. On my return from Okinawa we started out after a bad storm and experienced rough seas for what seemed like a very long time. In fact I began to wonder how long someone could live without eating. However, it all went away when we reached San Francisco and we all lined up on the upper deck as we went under the Golden Gate Bridge.

The LST's were a different story since they had a shallow bottom and rolled and pitched. Fortunately, I never had to take a very long trip on one of them.

One of my most interesting sea trips was passing through the Dardanelles on one of the largest sailing ships in the world, The Wind Star. This ship mechanically adjusted the sails without the help of ropes.

When I now read about the speed of "bullet" trains, size and speed of Boeing's Dreamliner and see the size of new cruise ships, I realize it isn't over yet.

Chapter 18

Reflections on My Retirement

During my years at Stevens, Thompson & Runyan, I had some excellent secretaries. They kept good records on which I have relied for much of what is written about the company. The rest has been my memory which is less reliable. Nevertheless, I have done the best I can.

I have been listed in Who's Who in Environmental Engineering and I am a life member of a number of professional engineering organizations. I stay connected through their monthly publications but even though I have a computer, I can no longer keep up with the unbelievable changes being made in the Engineering profession. Whatever happened to the slide rule?

It hardly seems possible that I have been retired for 33 years. I am extremely proud that the company I helped build continued to grow and was ultimately acquired by Jacobs Engineering, a large international consulting engineering firm founded in 1947. It has over 170 offices in more than 20 countries with operations in North America, South America, Europe, the Middle East, India, Australia, Africa and Asia. I still own stock in this company.

I feel very fortunate that my parents believed in the importance of education. My father had a grade school education and worked as a millwright in the paper mill. He introduced me to the possibility of Civil Engineering and encouraged my studies and my career. Little did he imagine then that all these years later the company I helped build would be recognized for key water and sewage projects not only in the Pacific Northwest but far beyond.

I have great respect for what travel has done for me during my life. It has been remarkable with regard to the people I have met, the friends I have made, cities, places and scenery I have witnessed. Most recently I took a weeklong trip with my family to Glacier National Park in Montana and Canada. I had never been there even though it is not a great distance from Portland. I was amazed by the grandeur of the Rocky Mountains and the beauty of the forests, lakes and wildlife. The glaciers are gradually melting and there are only 25 left. These are expected to be gone by 2030. This was a sad reminder that the earth is ever changing. I know there is a great deal more to this world than I have seen and I hope I will continue to have opportunities to see more.

At present my family includes my son Steve, his wife Jan, my daughter Nancy, her husband Randy, three grandchildren and seven great grandchildren. I have been fortunate to have Steve and Jan as my guides on many trips. Nancy has been a great help in the preparation of this book.

My travels have inspired my primary hobby of photography. I have made slide shows of all of my trips and shown most of them at Willamette View. At the Annual 2012 Leading Age Oregon Ageless Art Contest there were 121 entries from a number of retirement homes. My entry was a photograph I took in China in 2005. I won the Blue Ribbon Judges Award.

I continue to enjoy my friends, travel and photography and I look optimistically toward the future.

CPSIA information can be obtained at www.ICGtesting.com
Printed in the USA
BVOW011710021212

R4908800001B/R49088PG306849BVX1B/1/P